First published in October 1992.
Created and produced for Ediciones B, S.A.
by o3 BCN Packagers.
Text: Albert Delmar
Translation: M. Oliver
Illustrations: F. Salvà

© 1992, Ediciones B, S.A.
Rocafort, 104   08015 Barcelona (Spain)
All rights reserved.

ISBN: 84 - 406 - 3120 - 0
Depósito legal: CO 1023 - 1992
Printed and bound in Spain

Cover:
Self-portrait (?) (1623)
Oil on canvas (66x39 cm)
Museo del Prado, Madrid

U.S. & Canada Sole Importer/ Distributor
Trans-National Trade Development Corporation
New York City
Toll Free: (800) 592-2209
Telephone: (212) 922-0450
Fax: (212) 922-0462

Printed by Graficromo, S.A.
Córdoba (Spain)

VELAZQUEZ

A painter at Court

The story of Diego Velázquez

This is the story of a very important Spanish painter who lived four hundred years ago. His name was Diego Velázquez. He was born and grew up in Seville, a beautiful Spanish city full of color.

At school, Velázquez was a good student, but what he liked most was drawing and painting. When he was 10, his parents sent him to the studio of two famous Sevillian painters for training: Herrera and Pacheco, from whom he very quickly learned all the secrets of the profession. Pacheco was a very kind man, and Velázquez became his friend and visited his studio very often. Velázquez really had a great time there, and it was during one of these visits that he met Pacheco's daughter. The two of them fell in love and got married. Pacheco was very happy about the wedding, because this way he would always have his favorite pupil nearby.

When he was 24, Velázquez traveled to Madrid to paint a portrait of the young Felipe IV, King of Spain. He painted a wonderful picture, with the young king on horseback.

The king was so happy with the portrait that he appointed Velázquez court painter and they became close friends. From then on, Velázquez lived in the palace, where he always felt at home, just like another member of the court. He earned a lot of money and was served like a great master. And all for doing what he loved the most - painting!

When he was 30, Velázquez met Rubens, the famous Flemish painter, who was in Madrid fulfilling an assignment from Princess Isabel. Influenced by him, Velázquez made his first trip to Italy to learn from the great masters there.

9

Old woman frying eggs

Velázquez painted this picture when he was 19. At that age, he was already a great artist! It is a beautiful canvas.

   The food and utensils shown in the painting lead us to think that, at the time that Velázquez painted it, people worked in farming, livestock and crafts. Few children went to school. Most of them had to help their parents with the farm chores or with manual labors.

   The first thing that attracts our attention is the small round casserole with two fried eggs inside. Their shape and color almost make you want to eat them!

   The old woman couldn't be more real - her tired face, the folds of her skirt, her slightly curved back...

Old woman frying eggs (1618)
Oil on canvas, 39x66.5 inches
National Gallery, Edinburg.

11

In her left hand, another egg waits its turn. Perhaps it is for the boy looking hungrily at the casserole. But the grandmother looks at him placidly, as if to say "Wait a minute, they aren't ready yet."

Look how pretty the white scarf covering the old woman's head shoulders is!

As you can see, she is cooking at the hearth. All of the objects surrounding her tell us so: the oil lamp hanging from the smoky wall, the wooden table near the fire with the mortar, the bowl for the soup…

A little secret - the old woman in this painting was Velázquez's mother-in-law!

The surrender of Breda

This large painting is known all over the world as *The picture of spears*.

   With this painting, Velázquez celebrated Spanish military glory by remembering the defeat of the city of Breda, now located in Holland, in 1625. Although Spain's power had begun to decline, the court painter remained pledged to exalt the imperial powers over those territories which were under the dominion of the Spanish crown.

The picture of spears or *The surrender of Breda* (1635)
Oil on canvas, 121x144.5 inches
Museo del Prado, Madrid.

14

In the background, a cloudy, almost transparent sky. A little closer, the battlefield, with signs of recent combat. Velázquez painted this landscape without ever having been there, guided only by what others had told him. In the foreground we can see the heroes of the action.

Many of the faces are portraits of important persons of that time. If we observe them carefully, we can see who are the conquerors and who are the conquered in this battle - the facial expressions and the way the spears are held are quite different on each side.

In the center of the painting, a small object is the star of the composition - the key to the city of Breda, which Justino de Nassau hands to Ambrosio Spínola, the Genoese chief general of the Spanish troops, in symbol of his surrender. General Spínola, in turn, in a kind gesture, stops the defeated general from kneeling before him, as was the custom on these occasions.

18

Spínola's portrait was most probably painted from memory, since Velázquez knew him well - he had sailed with him from Barcelona in his second trip to Italy.

By the way, did you notice the man with the clear forehead standing near the horse, as if he is looking "at a camera"? What a look of satisfaction!

At the age of 50 Velázquez made a second trip to Italy, this time with the objective of buying works of art for the Court.

During this trip, which lasted more than two years, he visited the main Italian cities, made great friends and met many painters and important persons of the time, such as Pope Inocencio X of whom he painted a wonderful portrait.

Upon his return to Spain, he was appointed Palace Landlord. Due to the obligations of this title (among other tasks, he had to organize the Court ceremonies), Velázquez painted less and less. But this did not keep the few paintings from this period from being authentic masterpieces.

In gratitude for the services he had rendered, King Felipe IV named Velázquez Nobleman of the Order of Santiago, thus fulfilling one of his dreams - to be a member of the aristocracy.

The maids of honor

This is Velázquez's most well-known painting. He painted it when he was about 50. The whole world considers this family scene to be a masterpiece - a beautiful painting, yet, at the same time, very mysterious. Many people have spent hours and hours contemplating it.

On the left, there is a very elegant painter dressed in black, with long hair and a groomed moustache. He looks pensive. Can you guess who he is? It is Velázquez himself! What is he painting on the huge canvas in front of him? Surely it is a portrait of King Felipe IV and Queen Mariana of Austria, who we can see reflected in the mirror at the back of the room.

The maids of honor (1656)
Oil on canvas, 122x108.7 inches
Museo del Prado, Madrid.

The blond child in the center of the painting is Princess Margarita, daughter of the King and Queen of Spain.

Kneeling to her right, a young maid offers her a tray with a small reddish jar and is saying something to her.

But the little princess is distracted looking at her parents posing, and surely does not hear her.

There is an open door at the back of the room, where José Nieto Velázquez, the Palace Landlord, looks upon the scene.

In addition to the maids of honor (which was the name given
to the ladies-in-waiting), Princess Margarita and the midgets
Maribárbola and Nicolás de Portosanto are accompanied by
the governess Marcela de Ulloa and another nameless person.

There were also pets in the palace, such as the big strong dog we see lying in the foreground.

About to lose his patience, the old dog bears the mischievous midget Nicolás' teasing.

The Topers or The Triumph of Bacchus (1626-1631)
Oil on canvas, 66x75,2 inches
Museo del Prado, Madrid

Equestrian portrait of Felipe III (1633)
Oil on canvas, 120x125,6 inches
Museo del Prado, Madrid

Don Sebastián de Morra (1643-1644)
Oil on canvas, 42,4x32,4 inches
Museo del Prado, Madrid

Diego Rodríguez de Silva y Velázquez

1599 Born in Seville, son of a Portuguese father and Sevillian mother.

1609 At the age of 10, he spends a few months at the studio of Herrera el Viejo.

1610 He begins his apprenticeship under the painter Francisco Pacheco.

1617 He passes the Sevillian Painter's Guild exam.

1618 In April of this year, he marries Juana Pacheco, his mentor's daughter. Some of his painting of naturalistic themes and chiaroscuro treatment are from this period - *Old woman frying eggs, Christ in the house of Martha and Maria, The three musicians, Two young people eating, The water seller of Seville, Emaús' dinner, The Adoration of the Magi.*

1622 He travels to Madrid to paint a portrait of the young Felipe IV, King of Spain.

1623 Summoned by the Count-Duke of Olivares, he moves permanently to the Court as the king's painter. Some mythological paintings are from this period - *The Topers, The orgy* or *The Triumph of Bacchus* as well as a series of royal portraits.

1628 He meets Rubens in Madrid.

1629 He travels to Italy. During his stay there, he paints *The forge of Vulcano* and *The tunic of Joseph.* He also does some sketches of the Villa Medicis.

1631 He returns to Madrid.

1634-35 He does some paintings for the rooms of the Buen Retiro Palace, among them *The surrender of Breda,* also known as *The picture of spears.*

The Venus of the mirror (previous to 1648)
Oil on canvas, 49x70,8 inches
National Gallery, London

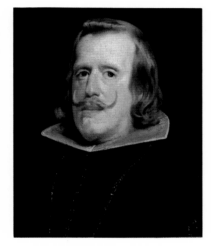

Felipe IV (1655-1660)
Oil on canvas, 25,6x21,5 inches
National Gallery, London

1643 He is appointed "valet" of the king. During this period he paints many portraits and the famous *Venus of the mirror*.

1649 He goes back to Italy a second time, staying there for two years. There his is appointed member of the San Lucas Academy in Rome. He paints several portraits, including one of the Pope, *Inocencio X*.

1651 Upon much insistence from the Spanish royalty, he returns to Madrid.

1652 He is appointed "Palace Landlord". He paints some mythological paintings, such as *The spinners* or *The table of Aracne*.

1656 He paints his masterpiece, *The maids of honor* or *The family of Felipe IV*, as it was known at the time.

1659 He is named "Nobleman of the Order of Santiago".

1660 On Pheasants Island, on the Bidasoa River, separating Spain from France, he attends the introduction of Princess María Teresa, Felipe IV's daughter, to her fiancé King Louis XIV of France. Soon after returning to Madrid, on August 6th, Velázquez dies.

Velázquez's paintings are principally located in:
Museo del Prado, Madrid, Spain.
Metropolitan Museum of Art, New York, New York, U.S.A.
National Gallery, London, England.

29

The Spinners (1657)
Oil on canvas, 66,8x100,8 inches
Museo del Prado, Madrid